Wakefield Press

IN THE ROOM WITH THE SHE WOLF

Jelena Dinić, who arrived in Australia in 1993 during the collapse of Yugoslavia, writes in Serbian and English. She is the recipient of the George Town Literary Exchange and The Arts Space residency in Rimbun Dahan, Malaysia, and the Eleanor Dark Foundation Varuna Writers' Retreat in the Blue Mountains.

Jelena is the co-editor of the Friendly Street Poets Anthology *The Infinite Dirt* and the author of two poetry chapbooks, *Buttons on My Dress* and *J Like Y*. Her poetry and short stories have been published in journals and anthologies including *Australian Book Review, Australian Poetry Anthology, Australian Poetry Journal, Best Australian Poems, Going Down Swinging* and *Westerly*, among others. *In the Room with the She Wolf*, her first full collection, was winner of the 2020 unpublished manuscript award at the Adelaide Festival.

When not writing poetry, Jelena is dedicated to working with students and families from culturally and linguistically diverse backgrounds (CALD), supporting their inclusion, settlement and wellbeing. She lives in the Adelaide Hills with her family.

IN THE ROOM
WITH THE
SHE WOLF

JELENA DINIĆ

Wakefield
Press

Wakefield Press
16 Rose Street
Mile End
South Australia 5031
www.wakefieldpress.com.au

First published 2021

Cover design by Stacey Zass
Edited by Julia Beaven, Wakefield Press
Typeset by Michael Deves, Wakefield Press

ISBN 978 1 74305 813 8

 A catalogue record for this
book is available from the
National Library of Australia

  Wakefield Press thanks
Coriole Vineyards for
continued support

For my grandparents

Contents

'Among the worlds, a world.'
Vasko Popa

'Међу световима свет'
Васко Попа

Swing

When my country collapsed, I was on a swing.
My mother shouted from her window 'hold on, hold on'.

J Like Y

1.

Nightmares don't stop just because you change your bed,
my grandfather shouted at the unhitched gate.

We have packed tomato seeds,
underneath our culture and language!

Anything to declare?
Yes, we have arrived!

2.

'Where are you from?'
'Yugoslavia.'
'Sorry, the country doesn't exist anymore.'
'Serbia?'
'No, it is not on our list yet.'
'What's the next one down?' asked a friend behind me.
'Siberia.'
'Good, put that one in.'

3.

'Can you spell?'
No. I know no magic.
But if I could
I would cast a spell –
change things back
to the way they were.

4.

'I have mail for you, love!'

'No love,' I say

snatching the letters

from this dangerous man on the motorbike.

5.

'Cross Cross.

Don't you understand past tense?

You *had* a house.

You *had* friends.'

6.

Remember the names:

Dragisa, Ljubisa

Dragoslav, Miroslav

Gustav, Fyodor or Anton.

7.

People think if they speak louder

I understand better.

8.

Remember the names:

Andrew, Nathan, Nigel, James ...

and a cool Serbian guy called Michael.

My name?

It half-rhymes with JFK's

inspiring speech to the people of Berlin
'Ich bin ein Berliner'.

9.
My new friend's name
Malsawmssanga.
Family name?
No family name.
Preferred:
Jeff.

10.
I cry in mother tongue
mostly in the library.
Open the first page.
Last page.
Back to the middle.
Shut it!
Make a mind map!
Make a mind map!

11.
How do you find again
things you left behind?
Obsessively repeat Popa's poems:
'Give me back my rags,

Give me when I ask you nicely.'
'The little box continues growing
The cupboard that she was inside is now inside her.'
'The little box remembers her childhood
And by a great longing
She becomes a little box again.'
'Let's see you find the world now.'

12.

At 20 I learn to laugh.

Knock, knock ...

Who's there?

Michael.

Michael, who?

13.

The overseas lines are breaking.

'May your children leave you, when you need them the most.'

My father fears his father's curse.

14.

I am falling in love with Adelaide

but Adelaide often tests my heart.

'Where are you from?'

I am a citizen of Berlin pops into my head.

'From here.'

'No, really, where are you from?'

Zahra's Page

Have you met Zahra?

Her babies know
Zahra is beautiful

with and without
her scarf.

Her Mother draws her face
like treasure lines on an empty map

then folds the paper the way
we fold away the thoughts of ourselves.

Zahra carries her burns
for the many of our fires.

The boxes on the form
are filled to fit Zahra's life.

Zahra doesn't want her life in a box.
She is fighting her way out.

She scratches at the insides of her eyelids
like a cat in the night.

She will run the same way
we dream of ourselves running.

If she stays alive this time
you might recognise her.

She will appear unexpectedly,
unveil herself and want you

to look into the mirror.
The mirror will show you everything.

The Shift of 90

1.

In a coal-coloured town
black fingernails scraping
bread of many layers.
They move
through the torch-lit crust.
They dig
Earth's dimples
deep into her mouth
until she widens
shaking, crumbling,
swallowing their breath.
Behind them,
day
breaks.

2.

With the shift of 90
the mine died.

The keeper guards the cemented hole
but from whom and from what?

3.

At the doorstep of
Palata Pravde
a tree had time to grow
young leaves
crushed and ground
under the boots and rain
in the just autumn.

Babysitting

For Mia

I wore my grandmother's clothes
and sat on her doorstep.
Monday to Friday.
She talked.
I lied.

'I'll teach you how to write,' I said
pretending I could
hold a pen.
'Mouse will eat your ears,' she smiled.

At night we leaned on pillows
watched TV with subtitles.
I made up foreign words.
I told her it was mostly German.

'Tell me more,' she said.
'Tomorrow,' I said
'Tomorrow is Saturday,' she replied.

Boudoir Grand

She opens its mouth to warm her body,
then takes off her cardigan.

Hands rise and strike the keys.
Broken ivory bones smell of elephants.

Only the sounds, hard and soft, violently repeat
like birds fighting for their prey.

I sit on the edge of a pillow filled with feathers.
Like an animal that needs to survive I sharpen my ears

and look up
at the music in the air.

Dancing Bear

You turn and wobble
in a drum
        drumming air
sticky mouths laugh
        clapping stings
a slap-stick
in master's hands
        straightens your step
beneath the patches of
moon and stars
        nowhere to run
with a terrible
beauty you reach
        for your bed and bowl
empty of a forest
        fairytales are quiet.

Katarisms and Dimstars

They talk
rubbing the light
out of their eyes.

'How much is 1 + one cloud?'
'You can't sum it, clouds don't make numbers.
They make pictures.'

'How do you know?'
'I've seen clouds looking like animals
and people's faces.'

'Look, we can almost touch them!'
Their arms reach high.
I pull them closer.

Passing

Winter brings new players to the table.
Wine in barrels, wheat counted
knotted fingers on the chessboard
playing the game by written rules.

Wine in barrels, wheat counted.
It is time to be inside
playing the game by written rules
moth hands around the lamp.

It is time to be inside.
One less player in the night
moth hands around the lamp
losing moves in a heartbeat.

One less player in the night.
Knotted fingers on the chessboard
losing moves in a heartbeat
winter brings new players to the table.

Hide and Seek

Children play hide and seek
hide when the siren howls
seek dead bodies after.

At the sparkles in the sky
people pray, make wishes
let the dog off its leash.

A mother tells her toddlers
fireworks are coming
but in her eyes fear grows.

Down in the basement
the fairytales
smell of mould.

In the Room with the She Wolf

All that is left is on the floor. Or is sailing
on the farmhouse dust

in waves of the washing cycle.
Hot and cold water, like a change of heart.

What passes through my hands is an old dress.
And that's when I feel best

the intimacy of death.
How it creeps into my head. Sets up a stage.

I am its guest and its host.
A thought quietly turns like a key.

Coming
closer

is this a girl who turned into me?
I circle her like an opponent.

Her clothes are still delicate.
I want to invite her to dinner.

She will step into my shoes.
Sit on my chair.

Her body will take my shape.
I know her weak spots.

I can't protect her from myself.
She will hang

disembodied,
in the backyard full of sun

and one of us will laugh.
There is no going back.

****

The land I left flowers in my dreams
picking my sleep out of its pattern
splitting stems from my roots

Crossing Borders

Your three sons
the most wanted.

One to protect
one to fight
one to celebrate.

Go give birth to them.

Bring them up.
Bring them back.

Blood Test

She calls my name, no mistake on her tongue,
double-checks my place of birth and
presses her thumb on my pulse.
We watch each other through needle eyes.
I am iron deficient and lack a plan,
but I sense we both have a fair share of bad blood.
I am Serbian.
Our grandfathers knew each other well.
They drew fences in medieval dreams
and said: 'Let there be war!'
She is too young to remember
but old enough to imagine.
'I am Croatian,' she says.
Once, in Croatia
I kissed a boy against the wall –
my confession from a heartland.
Then, silence –
delicate like a lowered flag hanging in the air
and long like a list of misplaced grandchildren.
The needle hooks into my vein as if
she is searching for the horror.
I let her have a sample.

Porcelain Doll

Careless hands took her travelling.
Tea parties and fairy lands.
Her doll face a map of storylines.

Still beautiful and fragile
like a teacup in the shaking hands
now trying to be careful.

Wedding

'Will you marry me?'
he asks.
'Yes,' she says
stepping on his foot
just in case.

Through the white lace
dreaming eyes
and a scent of frankincense.

Holding hands,
kneeling down
crowning their heads.

The life ahead
a fairytale – just
child's play.

My Sleep Walker

In the first third of the night
in sleep's deep slow wave

before eyes begin to dream
things happen.

I hear you.
The open-eye-night is looking for you.

It trespasses.
It lures you out to play.

You are eight.
In your eyes The Starship Enterprise.

The Death Star and Luke Skywalker
are missing a piece.

Balancing on the night's edge
you stretch your arms

towards a gang of stars
like a friend.

Darkness is spreading
my weakness across the night.

Moon mouth awaits with a glassy jaw.
Please, wake up. Wake up.

Icon

St Bartholomew's Church, Norwood

We enter small
like mice through the cracks of the church door.
In my hand, my daughter's hand,
I follow where she goes.

Between us the light dust. Icons gleam.
I face the saint on the glass window
where the sun rises with wings
and swords shimmer with sharpness.

For Him, our family bread
cross cut, kissed and turned around,
with hands passed on from father to son.

Now, a mother and a daughter
approaching slowly, remembering to fear.
To kneel, kiss and pray?

Instead,
I search for words to describe and define
the circle of life and the power of dust.

My angel asks: 'Who is our patron?'
'Someone who looks over our family,
watches over you.'

'*You,* Mum.'

My wings grow.
I kneel to her, I kiss her, I shine,
I carry my arms like a sword and a shield.

Behind the sunlight sharpness
I pray to be an icon in her eyes,
just a little bit longer.

Before and After

Chin up, Cleopatra eyes.
What do you like to hide?

Open your gates wide.
I see you smiling

in the hanging gardens of my mind.
Then the touch ups.

Your face pinned some place
beneath your concealer.

Packed bags in your dark circles.
In your glass vanity

masks are lined up
and suddenly,

it is all theatre
and every season autumn.

Alterations to the Little Black Dress

A little pin-up
three fingers
above the knees.

Behind the curtain
a dress-up game –
pretty things come undone.

He chalks lines
on raw stitches.
I catwalk.

My body fits the timeless black.
'You can live in it, or die'
smile the lips full of needles.

Do I look a little dead
with black fabric
on bone-pale flesh?

Suddenly in the mirror
I see the last party.
This dress is me.

In the front row
button-eyes watch
a grand entrance into
the handmade hole.

Around a little black dress
the roots of the earth
grow matching belts.

Handbag

After Vasko Popa

Always ready to leave
leaving
each time further
from the whispers
of the grass.

She has forgotten
her death,
the calf she once was.

Curled around an arm
a new name sewn
into her mouth
she's been there, done that.

A tramp, living beyond
the stitches of life.

****

With my eyes closed I learn your tongue.

It grows a whisper from your lips.

The Burning of the Dining Table

One day hunting
she catches the dining table.
It's been a fair chase for decades
but now the four legs had no choice.
She wants it to be an honourable kill.
In the name of a family
she pushes the beast out in the paddock,
starts the fire for a bigger feast.
The sky takes the last look.

The House

It stands on top of the hill
Like a portrait dressed in charcoal.
Welcome is a sign on a doormat.
I entered in white dress,
like a curious child, then
it was too late to run downhill.
Now, to see and to tell is a double dare.
Outside, the quince tree wears a net
like a dishevelled bride,
protecting its jewels
from the beaks of birds.
Only seasons change.
The house stands there full of itself.
The sight is driving me mad.
I don't forgive its certainty.
Its heart of stone.
At night I shut its glass eyes.
I light a candle
and fill the bathtub
but it's all ornamental.
The fire doesn't burn it
and water cannot sink it.
Only air is coming through the floorboards –
how it sounds like wheezing.
Like a fight for life.

Rainwater Tank

Rainwater
is sky's theatrical sobbing,
divulging itself,
extending an invitation
to the tank's throat.

To go there is family angst
fitting the gumboots
one of us must wear
when the grass gets dry.

In front of it
I am weak in the knees.
Myriad faces of me ripple
as I look through this
glass eye into the earth.

It is set in its foreign ways.
Will I know
to shout its language
when nature reignites.

Black bird burns
on the red rust sun
if not this summer
one will
spark the fear in the air.

The Water Factory

In the name of the family
the water factory
floats like a warship
reaching out its metal hooks
and nipping arms.
A wrong move catches a life.

Moulded sailors
climb up the ladder
in their plastic skins.
How many drops to kill our thirst?

They brush the copper tinsel crown
with the fallen nobility
of mass production
permitted to carry
one name
for the many faces
of us.

I Can't Tell You my Name

Call me princess
cold,
in the water tower.
'Move'
is a command
I practise a little
but if *I* do
I can drown in a drop
or go blind in its
perpetual gathered light.
Another message
is sent on a tray.
Stop asking for it.
I travel nameless
pure in the mouth.
I will kill your thirst.
Only for a little while.

Rimbun Dahan

Malaysia, November 2017

1.

I have not met the architect and his wife
but I am staying at their guesthouse.
It opens with glass and steel
to nature that is accepting.
A relationship based on truth.
The outside pool is the colour of jade.
Wrought flowers are rising above the surface
mirroring a Malay tribal belief:
Lord of Iron will eat the Earth to the end.
I find that loneliness grows in most suitable places.
A spare bed in my room is meddling with my mind.
A painting of hypnotic eyes hangs on the wall.
Tiny eye shapes of owls, or dogs. Or people.
It is 4 am. Prayers from a nearby mosque
are rippling across the jade water.
I watch the ceiling fan turning its rusty petals.*
I watch myself. The horror of letting go.

2.

I don't know the name of today.
It will be seen hanging somewhere
like a red tassel tied to a tree.
I wait for the monkeys to swing,
but the trees are still. Instead,
a bird flies into the roof
and screeches for freedom.
It is a sign, an ancient story.
The guesthouse opens like a lidded glass jar
but the bird doesn't see it yet.
It takes time to find a way out.

3.

I retrace my steps to the kitchen.
The scent of mint whirls above my teacup.
A sip at the time and I learn that
what binds us to ruins are gentle things –
like teardrops on chipped porcelain.
The bottom of the cup is glazed like the
belly of a fish. Struck with a spoon
it echoes the lost bells.
A slip through the fingers and the cup
will ring to the last peace.

4.

From the balcony of the guesthouse
the light swims across the jade water
and splashes the trees.
Monkeys didn't come out to play.
But yesterday, they were swinging
as if in the days of my mother's fear.
Hold on, hold on!

****

I wrote a poem
is whispered into an empty saucepan.
The secret echoes back.

Devil's Elbow

1.

It curves like a ribbon round the neck of the hill
then slides round its sides to the rib of the road.

I can get there with my eyes closed.

Wild and free – it is deadly.
In the fractured hour I turn into its tight grip.

Sometimes there is a poem there, or sex scene.
Words. Not real. Just written.

You prefer real?
Often, it is the only way.

2.

We speed on a HWY with the windows down.
'Romanian Rhapsody' is on the radio and
sunrays are playing hit and miss
across the windscreen.
You place your arm around my seat and
we turn to each other knowingly.
Departing is a daily rehearsal.

At night, we drive back
to tomorrow.
Sitting statuesque, headlights
defeated by the distance of roads
and slightly further from you
I am dream driving.
My bat-black hair is escaping
through the window.
All hair is dead.
This casualty is nobody's fault.

3.
Stop saying it is nobody's fault.
Words sound like staged collisions.

No broken bones, but the heart is not a bone.
If dislocated, it will be a long recovery.

You must be versatile.
Risk a turn. Drive back.

To days spent reconstructing
your mind, setting it in the right direction.

See if there is anything
in the dead-end street.

A resting point.
For now.

I watch you walk away –
not even a scratch.

You are welcome.

4.
Once I pulled over.
Watched a hitchhiker
under the light.

Where to?

From A to B
then back to me
was as far as I got.

5.
Steer yourself away from my line.
I am writing my way back.

All the vehicles are suddenly scrap paper.
I search them forensically.

At the intersection on South Terrace
I lean on the wheel and watch

the statue of a woman
a bling of promise in the sun

even if coming back
defeats the purpose of going forward.

This morning, there was a pillow on the grass.
Someone woke up and left.

6.
I trace the passenger seat and remember
my daughter measuring
how long until her feet reached the floor.

Driving from school.
The years.
The life lessons.

Forget France

We are here now. At our party
the oak tree is green in January heat
and you hope there will be no wind.
The branches all agree
even when you cut them
they come together nicely
in a gentle burning fire.
You put some meat on the fire.
The neck of your favourite animal,
a fine cut that you are proud of.
And here I am with a glass of red.
A drop of the best grape
proving how the cellared
rise to the occasion
only to drive you crazy.
I glance at the calculated position
of the furniture.
The old clock's glory is restored.
Its hands precise like an assassin's.
At the perfect interval
I will take my breath and turn to you
with a smile.

The Treachery of Images

1.

You write to remember it, but pages are missing.
There must be a reason.

You don't know how it happened.
He doesn't know either. It was his first time.

When he calls your name,
the sound of it singles you out

and the space bends you
down to him. Did you exaggerate?

You can't tell why the walls are crumbling
as you cross the corridor to your baby crying.

You kneel beside the cot and the scent of pink
reminds you to say: shh grown-ups pretend.

From there you watch the sun pulling itself up into the sky
and the light bleeds in your eyes with potential

but you doubt your days ahead.
The soft muscles of clouds will soon turn darker.

The bedside mirror will catch you in its glass eye
with sharp silence, a mutual gift. Look at this face.

You repeat your name in the mirror.
From time to time it helps you adjust the smile.

2.

Your voice in my poem
has a noble threat of metaphors.

The silence is a slow walk upstairs.
First steps are doubtful. A little push

goes both ways. I remember the mountains –
lost in a fog until you called my name.

We climb. You lead.
Your rightness echoes the walls.

I hold your hand,
holding back – the heart drawing

then erasing, the paper
clouding my vision.

A layer of dust falls
as if the walls are undressing.

Right there, we settle
for the step more difficult, but magical –

tricksters stripped of illusion
our mouths kissing the worst.

3.

My finger traces your spine
in a fine cobra shape

We lie on the grass –
between us the afternoon sun.

I am earthbound
humming the tune of charmers. And many emerge.

The baskets on bicycles hang innocently – and
those who are close walk home hand in hand.

The last flute-like coil of your body
makes me move

around the curves of thoughts
like a woman who could let a snake out of the basket

but the snake
will have a mind of its own.

Hotel Room Nightmare

We fly high to find the lost.
Outside, the last bits of clouds.

Illusions of faces and places.
No breathing spaces left.

I wear a dress out of the suitcase.
He buys us time at the Grand Millennium.

Behind the brass hotel door
with others in identical rooms

we unpack two hearts
we forgot we had

and let them bleed their weight
down the sliced floors.

I watch him gasping for air.
He watches me too.

****

On tables
the last round of brandy
served raw

Reading

I can't write letters.
I write leaves

in the water
in the sky
in the wind

and you do read what I write
you read with your skin.

Bargain Deals

I sit on the bench, next to a homeless man.
He smells like a day in my grandfather's vineyard.
The bluestone dust on his shoulders.
Copper sulphate burns his clothes.

Where I came from
death was a season –
we shot birds to save the grapes.

My grandfather used to say:
'Death doesn't do deals.
It looks around and takes its pick.'

I watch the homeless man
closely, like a bird.
I want to smell him better –
the sweat between his wrinkles.

He is at home in his skin.
We say no names.
No cheap exchange.

But I watch him
until I find in my mind
the vineyard way

taking small steps back
for a short visit.
If only

a bird for a grape
would bring the dead back.

Letter from Vera

It is the fountain pen, her retirement gift
that she uses to describe snow.

A shadow
falls from her hand and

follows
line

after
line.

She compares children on the street
to my children whom she will never know.

The last Christmas letter
is a smudge *With love.*

She prints her name
seals the absence.

Visiting Hours

Her door slides open
onto a make-believe passage

a yellow bus stop sign
placed for rehearsal.

Her performance –
a handkerchief

waving a welcome
to the final act.

Then, she bows to the bench
and listens

for someone
to arrive.

The Silence of Siskins

For my grandfather

He circles my arrival
on the calendar.

It is late November
and it doesn't snow.

A wooden pallet
hardens his bed.

He dreams of grandmother.
He doesn't want new dreams.

Two siskins in cages –
their song frozen like the air

that other November
when she lost her heart

cleaning and baking
for those who might arrive.

Above the fireplace a few flies
are nervous company.

'Not easy on earth,' he says,
'not easy below.'

Scrapbooking

He layers
memories on pages
scissors
his reflection
hangs it
in the air.

On a rainy afternoon
he closes
paper pores
with pins
glues
the sun
over him.

Cemetery Wear

I stand on the lands
of the dead

here lies the man
once dear to my hands

black dress granite
on my shoulders

white pearls
teardrops

delicate
as dust.

The Principle of Forgetting

Two crows fly
in front of the summer storm.
We hurry to the cemetery.
My father leads the way.

The stone garden has grown.
Through the maze of graves
we arrive, just in time

to unpack our silence
and let a few words
smooth their meaning
against the life.

Below my grandfather's name,
an empty space.
The year of death,
so neatly missing.

It has no possibilities.
Just weight.
A thought on my father's mind.

He explains the principal of forgetting.
The wind blows artificial flowers
across the graveyard.

We shelter the bread
so the crows can dine with the dead
then looking up,

we taste the rain like forgiveness.

I Didn't Answer Her Phone Call.
I Didn't Call Her Back

The last time we spoke I snapped at her sugared thoughts of
  happiness.

I said no, it's more about the miserable bits. For example, how
  many nights I can go to bed, asking myself so *what about it?*

My thoughts caught in waves of traffic, blurred by lights and
  rain. I sent a message to her phone *please, can someone let me
  know where my mother is?*

In the kitchen she is preparing for those who will come to take.
  Her food on my dining table, most days. Now the last bits
  remain, just the bones.

When she brought me a cake and made a wish, it wasn't my
  birthday.
The wish stuck like melted sugar.

I don't want all my mother's wishes to come true.
The cake resembles fragility. The icing is so pink it irritates
  me.

In a dream my teeth are peeling from the crown to the root –
  the layers of bone tissue turn into white petals.

I have used my teeth as weapons. Once, hungry like a fox, I
pulled apart a chicken on the table. I broke wishbones to
predict wars. Now I just bite my lip.

At the hospital, the nurse hands me a list of objects out of
place: my mother's watch, her wedding ring and her phone.
She says bones are treatable.

Her bones are broken and coiled inside her. Metal ropes hold
her body together.

I am holding her hand. The Serbian lullaby in my head has her
voice.
I lean to listen to her heart – it is beating the years I kept
myself away from her – unlearning family recipes, burning
my tongue, cutting my fingers, adding salt to her wishes.

Dear Words,

Please, find forgiveness
in your meanings
that I borrow without asking,
find the heart in your letters
to pardon me.

I trap you in a poem
like amber spiders in its light
transparent, helpless
beautiful inside.

I line you up, my precious words
and we follow each other blindly.
Wisdom grows as I steal
secrets from between your lines.

And one day when I take you all
to where the page ends,
when I close my eyes
with contentment at your count,
you will, my handmade art,
come back to me
all off by heart.

Song of Nothing

The old song hurts more when I play it in my head

The Head: A silver hole full of you

The Eyes: I see you but I don't trust you I see

The Old Song: Shut yourself and wait for me to drive you mad

Dead End: It is all in my head

The Head: Should have listened to a bird's song or a fly on the wall

The song is in the head. You are in the song.
The song is I. I am you.

Each season there must be a new you.
A new favourite you.

✳✳✳✳✳✳✳✳✳✳✳✳✳✳✳✳✳✳✳✳✳✳✳✳✳✳✳✳✳✳✳✳✳✳✳✳

Lost souls tangle
the air – their epitaph
the wind we run to

Back

Aleksinac, 2005

I walk through my hometown
as an uninvited guest.

Divorced
from communism

the old street has taken back
its maiden name.

I follow the steps of a lost child
watching myself

from behind the curtains
of memory's windows.

The doors of St Nicholas church
are rusty but open.

Inside familiar faces
and a sign

Buy candles here
they are blessed.

I count how many are needed
for the living

then for the dead.
The small flames

burn violently
in my eyes.

Snapshots

When I visit my village
only the water in the well
is still alive.

Icy, heavy water
pulses in the fertile fields,

fields that are christened
Markovo, Petrovo, Slavkovo ...

The old vineyards,
now cross paths with highways.
On the side grapes grow out of habit.

I remember the wine,
men dancing, pens behind their ears,
women in their arms.

I pose on the doorstep for a snapshot.

Voices utter from the walls,
'Where do you belong, child?'

Lamp-lit photographs are mute.
I pretend to know the answer.

Smile Like You Used To

I returned for
what I remembered was there.
But the house was as if broken into –
blank walls and empty drawers.
A few fingerprints on wine glasses
I find by chance
and I am guilty of not being there
to raise them.
A scarf, a green handbag,
an old dress
hung behind my daughter
who is taking a photograph
and tells me to smile
but, no. Not like that.
Smile like you used to.
She dresses up and giggles
and the house shakes a little
as if tickled awake. I walk
across the spine of a corridor
into my old room,
where a monster used to sleep.

Dining Table for Sale

Market is choking
on stories
collectors love to tell.

I carry a photograph.

Swimming in the Blue Caves

Adriatic Sea, July 2018

My children freestyle towards the beach –
they laugh and kick – don't even see the crab
that's holding for dear life onto a slippery rock.
They bomb-splash off the jetty.
How could you leave this place?
they shout in English,
their mouths full of flesh-biting salt.
They dive as if they are the offspring of a shark.

As a child
I crushed shells with teeth
and swam in the blue caves
with my eyes open.
Now I see in front of me
that the islands, like survivors,
keep their heads above water.
Their stone rooms have been rinsed into hotels
where movie stars stay the night.

The children's question ripples inside me
until I cut it loose from the layers
of my blue soul.
When it's gone,
I reach for the towels
and watch my children swim back
with the light that migrates
turbulently
across the surface of the sea.

The Sea Fever

A fisherman with one arm
throws a floating cage to capture the fish.
We walk on the jetty that slips into the water.
This blue day ends at the sea where it all began.
You flash under the glassy sun.
I wear my coral dress – a defence mechanism.
This is a sea fair. Golden bodies. Elegant species.
Everything thrown at us is fun to chase.
Children tiptoe around their perishing castle.
There are no great explosions to prove our wrong
moves.
We don't speak of dynamite, or the depths of the sea.
The remains of summer are buried in sand.
We watch the fish caught in a floating cage.
Precious few break out of it.

Notes

In the poem 'J like Y', the lines *Give me back my rags/Give me when I ask you nicely* are by Vasko Popa, translated from Serbian by Anne Pennington.

The quotes about the little box in the same poem are from 'The Little Box', 'The Tenants of the Little Box' and 'Last News about the Little Box' from *Homage to the Lame Wolf: Selected Poems 1956–1975* by Vasko Popa, translated by Charles Simic.

'I sharpen my ears and look up at the music in the air' (from my poem 'Boudoir Grand') is an image from the poem 'The Frequency' by Michael Symons Roberts. *It strikes a note too high for us,/though animals with sharper ears/do look up at the song and lean for cover./ You are a prisoner of rhythm.*

'Rainwater Tank' is written after reading poetry by Tomas Transtromer, especially the poems 'Looking through the Ground', 'Further In' and 'Sketch in October'.

The lines *I watch the ceiling fan turning its rusty petals./I watch myself. The horror of letting go* in the poem 'Rimbun Dahan' is after Mike Ladd's poems 'Bedroom Ceiling Fan' (*In winter/ it lies still/a three-petalled flower of ice*) and 'A Book of Hours at Rimbun Dahan' (*I start the great four-bladed ceiling fan./Seconds later a gecko drops to the floor, stunned./Yes, the world's like that./ We all hang on as long as we can*) in the poem from his book *Invisible Mending*.

Acknowledgements

This collection has its foundation in Serbian literary tradition and Eastern European style and culture, but the writing journey of these poems has been long enriched by Australian poets; their knowledge, talent and creativity.

I am indebted to Kate Llewellyn for linking arms with me and showing me the world of words as it is and what it could be. To Alison Flett for her magic editorial touch, friendship and encouragement since my first poem in English. To my mentor, Mike Ladd for his understanding and clarity when my words were caught between the languages. To Jane and Jason at the Halifax Café for supporting Adelaide poetry community. Some of these poems emerged from the night readings and the sparks that poetic minds create when they are together in one room. A warm thank you to those who influenced my writing with fine suggestions and creative opportunities: Peter Goldsworthy, Thom Sullivan, gareth roi jones, Jan Owen, Ken Bolton and Dr Valerie Volk.

My sincere gratitude to Writers SA and Georgetown Literary Festival in Penang for their generous support; and to Varuna Writers Retreat in the Blue Mountains and Rimbun Dahan Artist Residency in Malaysia for the time and space that is so precious to women writers.

A warm thank you to the Serbian Community in Australia for assuring me that while Serbia is far away it is never distant. To the Serbian SBS Radio and newspaper *Vesti* for their support of my adventures in journalism.

To legendary Socceroo coach Mr Rale Rasic for delightful conversations and for sharing his wisdom on life.

To my parents and to my sister and her family for the stories at the dinner table. To Dimitrije and Katarina, my guiding stars, and to Michael for making this journey worthwhile.

Thank you to the judges for selecting this manuscript for the 2020 unpublished manuscript award, and to Michael Bollen and Julia Beaven at Wakefield Press for a wonderful collaboration.

Printed in Australia
AUHW021525070622
364683AU00008B/22

9 781743 058138